I0071713

Lee Lister is a IT and Business Consultant with more than 25 year's management and consultancy experience and 20 year's program and project management experience in projects for many household names.

On the internet she is known as
"**The Bid Manager"** or
"The Biz Guru".

After owning her first profitable business at age 11 years, Lee Lister began an unparalleled journey through business consulting that continues to span across the United Kingdom, United States and the globe. Lee learned at an early age to identify a market need, such as the time when she a youngster in the small town of Clacton-on-sea, England, where she saw tourists arriving by the busload with no way to transport their baggage to the hotels. Lee had her father make a barrow that would hold enough luggage to charge a pretty penny while helping out the tired tourists at the same time. Hence, her first niche market was established!

She went on to work in or for a considerable number of different companies all over the world. Specialising in business change management and start up consultancy, her assignments included problem solving and trouble-shooting for companies suffering from inefficient business environments.

Lee has been published in several British and Asian industry magazines. She was recognised by an invitation to be keynote speaker at the International Business Development Conference in Washington, DC in 1997. She is highly skilled in lectures and corporate presentations on project management and bid management. In addition, Lee's experience in marketing and internet marketing are highly sought after. She is a prolific published writer of books, ebooks and articles and can easily be found on major search engines.

First published in Great Britain in 2008. Previous incarnations were part of an eBook.

ISBN: 978-1-907551-04-8

Other books available include:

Proposal Writing For Smaller Businesses
Profitable New Quilting Business
Profitable New Face Painting Business
Profitable New Bottled Water Business
Profitable New T Shirt Printing Business
Profitable New Cake Decoration Business
Profitable New Manicurist Business
How Much Does It Cost To Start A New Business?
Consultants' Tool Box

The Entrepreneur's Apprentice

www.StartMyNewBusiness.com

"You cannot keep determined people from success.
If you place stumbling blocks in their way, they will use
them for stepping-stones and climb to new heights."
Mary Kay Ash (1918–2001)
Saleswoman and Entrepreneur

This book is dedicated to my daughter Kerry Lister for whom I have always strived to be my best.

CONTENTS

We do not believe in get rich quick schemes. We do believe that success is equal parts of inspiration, hard work and luck. Every effort has been made to represent accurately our product and it is potential.

Please remember that each individual's success depends on his or her background, dedication, desire, and motivation. As with any endeavour, there is an inherent risk of loss of capital. **There is no guarantee that you will earn any money or obtain a new job**.

This book will provide you with a number of suggestions you can use to aid your chances for success. **We do not and cannot guarantee any level of success.**

This book is written with the warning that any and every venture contains risks, and any number of alternatives. We do not suggest that any one way is the right way or that our suggestions are the only way.

You read and use this book on the strict understanding that you alone are responsible for the success or failure of your decisions relating to any information presented by our company Biz Guru Ltd.

Starting a New Business?

Every entrepreneur, to achieve any amount of success should be motivated. Motivation is always difficult to maintain. You are working all hours of the day, rarely see your family and friends and are so stressed that you could just...... Yes, I have been there - many times actually. The times when you cannot get to sleep worrying about when you pay the next bill, when your key member of staff does not turn up and you have to drop everything and rush to your business. Maybe you just do not have enough money to market your business so you cannot move to the next level. Worrying is not it?

However, it does not have to be that way - sure, I cannot make your staff turn up - but this book CAN help you inspire and motivate them so that they turn up and work as best they can.

I cannot pay your bills, but this book CAN show you how to make your business more efficient so that you get a good night's sleep.
This book CAN show you how to get your company known and your sales up with a very small budget, some ingenuity and a bit of hard work!

So maybe you are just starting out with your business, just got a great idea and not sure where to from here?

The First Steps

It is as easy as 1, 2, 3 err 4! It is a fact that some people are not content with their current job and are looking for more challenges but are wary of the loss of security this may entail.

Many others have that urge to start a business but are not sure when, where and how to make the jump to relying upon themselves.

Starting out a business can seem overwhelming. Issues such as what you really want to sell, the legal technicalities of starting up a business, developing your business and marketing strategies and building that all important, customer base are just some of the initial obstacles entrepreneurs face. Here are 4 steps for you to follow.

Step 1: Form and define your ideas

Work out what you want to sell, in what format and whom you want to sell it to. Find out what your potential competitors are doing and work out what you can do that is slightly different and preferably better. Talk to your friends and associates and get feedback – good or bad about your ideas. Look at other similar businesses in order to gain an appreciation of the market need for your idea and how large the market size is likely to be.

Once you understand the potential of your business, you should name your company and register it as a legal entity, obtain all the licenses that you need and do not forget your insurance – you do not want to lose your business and your life savings before you even start.

Step 2: Test your ideas

With small groups of potential buyers, ask them for feedback and ideas of how to improve them. Get a market stall or a booth in a shopping mall and hand out free samples in exchange for their comments – people loving being asked for their comments. The number of people who are happy to try your free samples gives you an indication of popular your product will be.

If you have a service, go to a conference and exhibition, get a small stand and offer your services at "introductory rates" or with added extras such as reports, books or training.

Look at all the different ways that you can pack your products or services. Maybe there is a market out there that you will discover as your test out your new business. Continually look for a niche market that you can jump into. A niche is a small market, usually with a dedicated following but with few suppliers. Many companies have made fortunes jumping into or making their own niches.

Before Dominoes - pizzas were never delivered. Before Tupperware you did not buy things at a party. Ford was the first business to mass produce automobiles. Get the picture?

Continually get feedback - good or bad - and ACT upon it. Make notes; refine your plans, your products and your market as you go along. Look at how you sell and package them, where and when the best place to sell them is as well as your pricing structure.

Step 3: Define your strategies

With the aim of developing a loyal customer base, having an efficiently running business and retaining existing customers. Develop a Business Strategy that sells your products or services in such a manner that your cash flow and profits are maximized.

Make sure that your Business Model works. This means that your goods and services are designed, packaged and delivered in an efficient manner. You have just enough stock, your prices are at their most effective level, and that the costs of fulfilling each order are as low as possible.

Define your Marketing Strategy to ensure that you have differentiated yourself from the competition and made your products and services compelling and a necessity to your potential customers. Ensure that you have established your Brand that is how your customers will recognise your company, your products and what you stand for.

Once you have done this, formalize them all, alongside your financial needs, your market analysis and your company information in your Business Plan.

Most importantly, make sure that you stand out from the crowd, meet the needs of your potential customers and make a profit whilst having fun!

Step 4: Implement your strategies

Raise capital with your Business Plan and confirm the financial capabilities of your business. Set up your fulfilment route, that is, how you obtain your orders, how you manage your customers and how you deliver the end products to your customers. Remember that you also want to look after your customers after they have received your goods or services. Remember a happy customer will recommend your business and hopefully come back for more.

Remember also to set up such items as manufacturing, storage, packaging, transport and confirmation of delivery. If need be set up payment processing and banking facilities.

Set up your web site and telephones, offices and make sure that your staff are trained.

Set your marketing plan in motion and all the associated processes so that you can meet, greet and make your customers happy.

Remember, Review, Innovate and Improve.

Will Your Business Be Successful?

Should not you be the first to know? So you have a great idea, you are ready to be your own boss so how do you get started? Well sit down with a pen and paper - a few trusted friends also help and see if you have answers to the following:

Yourself

- Do you think that you have the skills necessary to make a success of running a business? These include the ability to work alone for often long periods and a great deal of perseverance.
- Do you get on well with people and do they think that you are great to talk to?
- Can you step back if need be and let someone else contribute to your business?
- Do you have good time management and are you able to prioritize your work?
- Are you able to see "the big picture" but still be able to see each individual item and action that makes up each individual stage?
- Do you have some financial stability?
- If your business is craft based or an offshoot of your business, are you also able to handle managing the business?

Your Ideas

- How is what you are offering different from what is already being offered by others? - This is your Unique Selling Point.
- Are there any legal, ethical or moral reasons working against your success?
- What kind of company do you want to run?
- How much of your time do you want to devote to your business?

- Do you have the skills and attitude to make the business a success?
- How will you make money from your business?
- Will you make more money than it costs to run the business?
- Have you made sure that you are not copying someone else or you are copying them?
- Is someone else doing the same thing but better?

Your Market

- Will it meet a real need or solve a problem?
- Whom are you selling to? Who do you think will be interested in your offerings?
- Will they want what you are offering, at the price you are asking?
- How much do you think they can afford to pay?
- How big is the market?
- What share of the market do you want?
- Can you establish a niche in this market?
- Who are your main competitors?
- How is the market changing? Is it shrinking, growing or changing?
- How will you tell people about your business?

Your Financing

- How much will your company cost to start and run for the first year?
- How will you raise the capital required and how much will you being contributing?
- Where will you raise it from?
- If you have investors or partners, how do you think they will get their money back and how long will it take to give it back to them?
- What risk is there that you will not get your investment in time and money back?
- Will you raise enough money to run the company through the first difficult year?
- Do you plan to sell your company or go public (list the company on the stock markets) one day? - This is your exit strategy.
- Anyone is capable of making a product, process, or technology better. Is not it time for you to become your own boss?

Your Business Framework

What Scaffolding Do You Need? When starting a business of whatever kind, large or small, there is always a framework or scaffolding that you have to set up. Not only does this make your business much more effective, but it also saves you from many embarrassing and costly problems. Here is your framework:

- **Business Name.** Choose an appropriate name that sums up what your business stands for. It has to be unique – try to ensure that a suitable domain name is also available, as you will probably want a web site. The owner of an established web site might cause problems if you give your brick based business the same name, so be careful in your choice.
- **Your Business Entity.** Obtain professional advice as whether to the best way to set up your business as a limited company, partnership etc. Then register your company.
- **Patents and Trademarks.** If you have unique products then you need to ensure that you have registered your patents before your start trading. Similarly, any product names, mottos, selling tags etc should be trademarked. Take professional advice on how to do this.
- **Licenses and Permits.** Ensure that you have all the licenses and permits that you are legally required to have.
- **Insurance.** You may think that you do not need this but you do and will. So take out property, business, vehicle liability, staff and disaster insurance. A good broker can advise you.

- **Taxes.** A necessary evil I am afraid. Register with your local tax collector. Set up a good accounting system and hire a good accountant.
- **Employment Laws.** Establish what you local employment laws are and ensure that you adhere to them. Set up employee guidelines and handbooks. Make sure you hire and fire legally.
- **Banking.** Visit your local banks and find the best business bank account and credit card for you business. Always keep your business and personal spending separate.
- **Business Plan.** This is your carefully written plan on how you want your company to operate, what you want to sell, where and to whom. It includes your business and Marketing Strategy as well as your financial standing and projections. This is the foundation of your business.
- **Liquid Cash.** Ensure that you have enough money to carry your through the first few months of your business as well as any foreseeable troublesome times ahead.

When you start up your business, remember to tick off the 10 items above and you will have a very sound start to your business.

How Much Does It Cost To Start A Business?

The most common question that I am asked! You have your business idea, think that you will be able to get a good loan and even have your Business Plan being written but.... The one big burning issue is – How much does it cost to start a business?

Well you first have to be realistic and understand that you are unlikely to make a profit within the first six months of business – so you should also budget for your first six months running costs. Therefore, here is your shopping list:

- **Purchase of lease, franchise, and premises**. This will include any Realtor fees, deposits and other legal expenses.
- **Cost of fit out and purchase of new equipment**. This will include any work that needs to be done on your premises as well as any equipment you have to buy in order to start and run your business. Often you can lease equipment in order to mitigate high start up costs.
- **Any loans** that you have will also have to be paid. Again, look at least at six months or until you break even and can pay the loan.

- **Six months worth of advertising and marketing.** This will be particularly high at the start as you establish your business. Factor in some cold calling as well as a launch party or opening day.
- **Stock and supplies** – to keep you going for six months.
- **Legal, licensing and banking costs.** Your business will need to be set up correctly, licensed and have a good bank account. Sadly, all of these require money. You may also need a payment processing service to use credit cards.
- **Staff costs for six months.** Staff will be the basis of providing good service to your new customers. Make sure that you have enough money put aside to find them, train them and keep them!
- **Uniforms, office and marketing supplies, packaging etc.** You will need to establish your Brand. This means that your staff will need uniforms or at the least business cards and nametags. You will need brochures, adverts etc. If appropriate, you will also need standardized packaging and documentation. Your office will also need office equipment and supplies. You should also budget for designing your logo, brochures and adverts if you cannot do this yourself.

- **Maintenance for six months** – your equipment will also need to keep going for six months.
- **Your salary for six months** – Lastly, you will need to pay your own bills and maintain your family during this time.
- **Contingency** - add this up and add 10% for contingency.

Business Planning

Unless you are very lucky, you will need investment to help you set up your business. Investors want a Business Plan before they will even discuss investment. However, even if you have money, every new business still needs a Business Plan. It helps you define your business, find your market and price your products.

Writing Your Business Plan

Nah! I can do that myself ...and why you should not.
There are three reasons why you need a Business Plan......

Reason 1: To obtain funding.
Every good potential lender or investor, be they bank, Angel Investor, venture capitalist or business partner, will require a Business Plan. They want to be comfortable that you have thought long and hard about your business rather than jumping straight into a business.

More importantly, they want to ensure that they have a good chance of not only having their investment returned, but also making a profit out of the arrangement.

Your Business Plan is your sales tool - it explains your business and your strategies to make this business a success. It shows how detailed and organized you are and how you intend to make a success of your business.

Reason 2: To introduce your business to potential funders.

The Executive Summary in undoubtedly the most important part of your Business Plan. Investors receive hundreds of Business Plans. They decide on their initial sort of who they want to investigate more thoroughly, by viewing the Executive Summary. Yours should be short, concise and eye catching. Investors like entrepreneurs who can concisely and accurately describe their business, products and potential. If you think of it, this is what an effective sales person does every day.

If your Business Model is not planned well enough to be able to describe in a few well-written pages then it is unlikely to be successful and very unlikely to be funded.

Once a potential investor has viewed your Executive Summary and become interested in your potential business, then they will read the rest of your Business Plan in order to gain a greater understanding of your business and investment requirements.

Your Executive Summary should be written after the main part of the Business Plan and should be no more than three pages long. It should summarize your Business Plan and include an overview of your business, your Business Models, what you are selling and in which market. You should also summarize your financial requirements and projections as well as provide your investor's exit strategy.

Reason 3: To ensure that you have a carefully planned business

A well planned business is a business likely to succeed. Do you know who your potential customers are? Do you really know whom they are, where they are and what they are looking to buy that you might be able to sell to them?

Do you know how to define your company within a sales environment? Where do you want your company to be in three years?

Do you know how many staff you will need? How you will pay for these staff?

Do you have a vigorous Business Model? Even know what a Business Model is?

Have you really thought through how you will run your business?

The answers to all of the above, plus many more will be discovered, decided and defined during the Business Planning process.

What Should be in your Business Plan

There are three key areas to your Business Plan:

1. **Executive Summary.** This should be an overview of the key factors of your main Business Plan as well as a memorable selling tool.
2. **Main body of narrative.** This should include your main information about your business, strategies, markets, products and staff.
3. **Financial information.** This should support the rest of the Business Plan and be strong and informative enough to support the loan or financing application.

The Executive Summary

This is your main selling tool and as the title suggests, should be a summary of your Business Plan. It is the part that your potential investor mainly looks at so make it compelling and memorable. Some graphics to explain more concepts that are difficult always helps.

The Main Body of Narrative

This should include the following information:

- **Your Company:** The structure, location and description of your company and its shareholders. Describe what buildings you will need to buy, rent or lease. You should include your mission statement and business objectives. Your Business Model should be clearly set out.
- **Goods and Services Offered:** This should include a brief overview of what you are selling, at what price. How they will be produced or manufactured and the deployment and fulfilment processes. An idea of the profits are possible should be included. The benefits that your customers will accrue from using your company as well as how you differentiate yourself from your competitors should be outlined.
- **Your Market:** Describe the market you are aiming for, its geographical location, size and demographics. Examine your competitors in these markets and how you will meet these challenges.
- **Your Marketing Strategy:** Define your Unique Selling Point (USP) and your Key Selling Points (KSP). You should also describe your Marketing Strategy and how you will be marketing and advertising your products and services.

- **Your Staff:** Identify the major managers and all the directors in your company. Define the different types of staff you will be employing as well as the numbers. An organisation chart and respective resumes should be included.
- **The Way Forward:** What the loan will be used for, where you see the company being in three and five years and the various Exit Strategies you have considered for your investor.

As with the Executive Summary, graphics to explain complex details is always a welcome assistance.

Financial Information

It is very important that your financials are believable and support what you have written in the rest of the Business Plan. Your sales should be achievable and should point towards a profit within a reasonable time.

The easiest way to present your financials is within a spreadsheet. This can be attached to your Business Plan or included within it. Your financial information should include:

- Start up costs.
- Sources and use of the funding.
- Capital costs and equipment.
- Opening Balance Sheet.
- Projected Income and Profit statements.

- Break-even analysis.
- Cash flow analysis.

You should give considerable detail for your first year and less detail for year 2 and 3.

Why Use a Business Planning Consultancy.

If you use a professional Business Planning company, you have the advantageous of not only having a well written Business Plan, but you also benefit from the business knowledge of the planning company.

A well written and thought out Business Plan will help you to clarify your own thoughts about your business, how you want to present your company to your peers, customers and investors.

It will help you find out who your best customers are, where they are, what they want to buy and at what price. It will identify any weaknesses you may have in your thinking.

Lastly, it will provide you with a business and Marketing Strategy combined with a robust financial model and Business Model that will give you confidence to make the leap into entrepreneurship.

A professional company will have experience of writing many different kinds of Business Plan for many different types of companies. A plan written for a Venture Capitalist is totally different to that which an Angel Investor or a bank requires.

A good Business Planning company understands this and how to answer the particular concerns of each type of investor or lender. They will pitch you plan to your potential audience.

Investors are risking their hard earned capital by investing in your business and they are entitled to be comfortable that you have a clear business strategy a robust Business Model and have researched your potential market in great detail. They also want to be comfortable that you understand all the risks that your new business faces.

Many business owners, who write their own Business Plans, often do not include all the information required or include information that is not required.

Many amateur plans are unfocussed and discuss information that is not required in detail. An unfocussed and unstructured Business Plan gives off the wrong impression that you are also unfocussed and unstructured.

To a new entrepreneur you will be very short on time – in order to produce a Business Plan you will not only need a great deal of time to produce the plan but will also need to take time on a steep learning curve.

A professional Business Plan company has climbed this curve and has enough experience to guide you through the whole process, set your mind working in the right direction and prompt your thought processes.

Your Business Plan consultant will be objective in reviewing your business and have the experience to offer suggestions and advice during the writing process.

Hiring a professional allows you to concentrate on finding and servicing your customers, although a good professional will involve you at every stage and your input is definitely required to ensure that the plan reflects YOUR business.

The money you pay for a Business Planning consultant will give you a quality, investor ready Business Plan with some very useful business consultancy as a bonus!

Investors in Your Business

You've got the great business idea, you are all set to start your new business - all you need now is some finance. So where do you find those elusive investors - or better still some no strings money?

When looking for investors in a new business first seek out any grants or government assistance that your state, county or country offer - as this money is often subsidized and easier to obtain for a new business.

Your next stop would be the bank. They will be seeking to lend you money that is secured on some kind of collateral. A business loan is more usually for 2 - 5 years. A bank will not generally want to get involved with your business - just some confirmation that they will get their money back with interest.

The next port of call is an investor. Now these people are totally different to banks - in that that are actually investing in you and your business and they often want to get involved with your business as well. So let us analyse this a little more.

What Do Investors Look for in a Business Plan?

Your Business Plan - the foundation of your business and the path to a business loan. So what makes a good Business Plan and what do investors look for in your Business Plan?

- **A realistic, viable business idea** that reflects extensive market research and includes a full analysis of the market and its relevant competition.
- **Motivation, credibility, financial responsibility** and investment from the owners and directors. If you do not invest in your business why should they?
- A **manageable amount of risk** that is compensated for by a profitable return.
- **A road map of goals, targets and milestones** that will lead to profitability and the ability of the investors to profitably leave the company within a few years.
- **A financial budget that reflects the capital requirements** necessary to fuel the operation through the start-up stage, make a reasonable return to the investor and allow for investment in future enhancements and product changes. The financials should include a break-even position, feasibility analysis and realistic profit forecast.

- **A comprehensive market analysis,** reflecting the demographics of the market, the demand for the product or service, who your competitors are and how much of a threat they are to you.
- **A Marketing Strategy** that will ensure that you penetrate the market quickly and position the company in a place where it can grow, capture market share and build your Brand.
- **A competitive advantage** that will meet the needs of a clear target market with stable growth potential.
- **A clear understanding of the company's structure and culture** as well as a clearly defined Business Model and strategy.
- **An overall attractive plan** that reflects profitable capabilities, stability, entrepreneurship, financial acumen and that will provide a high return on their investment in a foreseeable amount of time.

What are Investors Looking for in Your Business?

They want a sound business or business idea with some kind of unique concept that they believe will rapidly move to profitability. They want a well thought out and credible Business Plan with realistic financials.

In you, they want a hard working entrepreneur with good experience in the business area. They will look at your personality, your abilities and your past resume to see if you are the kind of person that can make a success of this type of business. Similarly, they will want to feel that they can work with you – because they will be.

Investors will only want to invest in your business for a few years, often a low as one year. They expect to be able to obtain a good rate of return on what they see as a risky investment. They will also often require a share of your business as their security. If you are seeking a large loan – they will often request a seat on the board of your company so that they can exercise some kind of control on the business activities.

What Will an Investor Bring to Your Company?

Experience and Guidance: Investors often invest in areas that they know a lot about. They are obviously keen for your business to be a success as their return on their investment is dependent upon this factor. This means that they will often offer guidance and help to you as part of the package.

Cash Injection and Cash Flow: Sometimes you can request a staged investment from an investor, subject to you reaching agreed deadlines. This not only concentrates the mind in your business development, but also ensures that money is available when you need it. Suffice it to say that cash is always welcome in a business.

Your Business Plan is very important. You need to prove that you meet all the requirements above, but you also have to include what is called an Exit Strategy.

This answers and lays out in detail, the four questions that every investor will ask:

- What is in it for me?
- How soon do I get my money back?
- How risky is it?
- How much will I make from this investment?

One last suggestion for you - if you have no actual experience of the business you are starting then try to get some working experience before you lay out on your business. This does not mean that you should steal from you employer – just learn.

Marketing Strategy and Plan

Whether you have a business based on the internet or the "real world". - Click or Brick - then you need marketing to ensure that people know about your business and products. After all, if people do not know about you they will not buy from you. Effective marketing accomplishes several things:

- Creates and maintains your business Brand.
- Highlights your Unique Selling Point (USP)
- Establishes your company as an authority.
- Introduces your products to your potential customers.
- Allows you to capture a niche in your market.
- Ensures that your business is remembered within your market place.

So how do you begin to design your business Marketing Strategy?

- Decide how you want your company to be recognised and remembered by your potential customers, customers, peers and competitors. This is your Brand.

- Decide what products you want to market and whom you think may need and want them. This is most important – people only buy if they perceive a need for them or you build up a desire for them. The latter is more lucrative but very expensive to do – but ask iPod how effective and profitable it can be.
- Investigate your potential market and define a niche within this market. A niche allows you to market to fewer, more responsive people. Not only cheaper but also more cost effective.
- Redesign and re-price your products as necessary. This is a recurring process.
- Establish your marketing budget. There are cheap ways to market such as viral marketing – but you will still need some kind of budget.
- Decide how you will market your business and products, how often and in what format. Nearly there.
- Set this all down in your Marketing Strategy.

Now go and market your business.

Marketing

The life blood of your business and the single most difficult thing to get right. Marketing is spreading the message about your business and products as opposed to directly advertising one or more products. Marketing can be expensive, doubly so if it is ineffective. If marketing is undertaken correctly it can bring staggering results. There are several types of marketing.

Grassroots Marketing

This is localised marketing, building a bottom up (grass root) awareness of your company. Marketing efforts include passing out fliers and coupons, or appearing as a guest on a local radio show as opposed to using paid radio advertising.

Grassroots marketing tends to use people to spread the word, such as referrals. It is heavy on legwork but light on costs and depends upon having a good message about your company that people want to pass on.

There are some great ideas on Inc.com, which includes the ice cream vendor who encourages her staff to break out in song or comedy routines, thus making a visit to her shop an occasion and encouraging visitors.

Guerrilla Marketing

This is a term first coined by Jay Conrad Levinson in his book of the same name – *Guerrilla Marketing, 1984*. A book that should be on every entrepreneur's bookshelf. This type of marketing is unconventional and very low budget and successful campaigns are always talked about. The concept is to create a *"buzz"* about your company or products such that news about your campaign and hopefully your products as well are spread exponentially. The term has since entered the popular vocabulary to also describe aggressive, unconventional marketing methods.

One such method, that is now big business in Japan, is Tissue Marketing, where tissue packs are handed out to commuters and passers by.

The tissue pack contains a marketing message. This is a low cost way of getting your marketing message into the hands of your potential customer. It has been found to be far more effective than handing out flyers, which are often quickly discarded.

Viral Marketing

This is marketing that uses existing social networks in order to increase Brand awareness and knowledge about your products and services. It facilitates and encourages people to pass along a marketing message voluntarily. Viral promotions may take the form of video clips, interactive games, ebooks, images, jokes, or even messages. The basic form of viral marketing is not infinitely sustainable so you will need to continually send off your message and have multiple examples circulating at the same time.

The popularity of social networking web sites have increased the ease of Guerrilla Marketing, by the use of humorous clips, but now, of course, you have to fight that much harder to be noticed.

Conventional Marketing

With Conventional Marketing, you have a whole arsenal of marketing techniques at your disposal. These would include:

- **Media Promotion** such as appearing on TV, radio or print.
- **Press Releases** to announce important events in your business life such as winning an award or launching a new product.
- **Article Writing** so that you appear in print in magazines and on other web sites.

- **Flyers and Brochures** being handed out to prospective customers.
- **Seminars and Talks** that promote you as the expert.

Branding, The How's, What's And Why's

In order to be successful in marketing, you need to have a strong identity and business Brand to promote. Your business Brand says a lot about you and your business. If you create a strong Brand image, it will elevate you above your peers and provide a good model for your product and service development as well as a sound foundation from which to expand your business.

So what is Branding? Many people think that having a logo and maybe a short description of their services is all they need to set up their Brand. This is not so. Your Brand encompasses all that your business does, from first contact with your potential customers through to how your products are defined and sold.

Your Brand is what defines and describes your business. Look at any two different companies that compete in the same market and look at how people recognise and remember them.

For example look at Rolls Royce and Toyota - they both sell cars but each company is known for a different reason. Someone looking for a car on a budget would not go to Rolls Royce - yet both sell their cars on reliability.

Clearly more people would aspire to purchase a Rolls Royce, but many are also happy to purchase a Toyota.

Look again at the perceived value of a Brand. Why is the iPod the desired MP3 product when other Brands have similar properties and reliabilities? People perceive the iPod to be superior and are willing to pay more for the pleasure of owning one. Indeed many people would not consider any other purchase. This is clever Branding by Apple who marketed their product as being very desirable to certain markets.

I Do not Have that Kind of Money - So Why do I Need to Create my Own Brand? The main reason has to be to differentiate yourself, but it also makes the promotion of your company and development of your products so much easier. There are thousands of new businesses and many times more web sites. You need to:

- Set yourself apart from the competition
- Make yourself memorable so that people will either look for your business or choose you above your competitors.

- When introducing your business to a new customer, your Brand should go before you and communicate much of what you want to say.

Your products are easier to define and design, if you centre them on your Brand definition. For example, we have PowerPacks that include everything you need to set up a specific type of business. We take this concept and produce the products to fit this Brand image. We are known for our PowerPacks that helps with our sales.

So How Do We Create Our Own Brand Then? You Brand must say:

- Who you are
- What you do
- How you do it
- What the benefits of using your business are

You Brand MUST establish your company and build your credibility with your prospective customers.

In order to be able to do this you must first be able to describe what you want your business and products say, so start with your Mission Statement or Elevator Statement.

- **The Mission Statement** - this is what you want your business to be or do as it operates. You need to be realistic and focused. Being profitable is not a mission statement, but deciding what you want to do to be profitable is.

- **The Elevator Statement** - This is 1-4 sentences that you would use to describe your business, in the time that it takes to travel in an elevator - or a few minutes. It is used when meeting new people who ask "and what do you do?" or as an introduction when networking.

So What Should Be Described Within My Brand? First, pretend that you are one of your target customers and list five things that they will be seeking from your product. These items would encompass a short definition of one of more of the following:

- Price
- Quality
- Service
- Support
- Components of the product
- Scarcity or availability
- How and when delivered
- Accessibility
- Security

I am sure that you can think of a few more that relate to your business. So now define who, what and where you are in these terms and you should come up with something like this....

"We provide some of the hottest business and marketing informational products on the internet and all of our products are of the highest quality. Most of them we write ourselves or we scour the internet and read every book that we sell, to ensure that they will be useful to you as well as good value."

This is the mission statement of our informational product part of our business - selling under the Brand name Clikks.com

We have defined what we are selling, to whom and established our credibility as well as providing an easy to remember and catchy Brand name.

Is That All Then? Not quite - you now need to be recognised by your customers. Here is where you tag line and logo comes into play.

My tag line - what is that? Well if you become as well known as Nike it can be something very short like "Just Do It" - but that is a few years and few $million down the road. Your tag line is a short description of what you do.

Something like "Consultancy Information and Services for the Serious Entrepreneur" which explains what we sell and to whom. It also differentiates us from the many less than appropriate sellers of business information.

Now you need a logo - it does not need repeating that this should also reflect your Brand. If you are saying you are modern and efficient - you do not want an old fashioned, messy looking logo. It should always reflect your Brand and be simple and recognizable.

You should include it on:

- All your communications.
- Your web site.
- Your products.
- Your give aways.
- Your marketing materials and adverts.

Yes, Got All Of That - Any Last Suggestions?

Be consistent with your Brand promotion - do not keep changing it as people are more likely to remember things the more they see them. Regular marketing enables you to establish your credibility and relevance to your target market. Remember your Brand allows you to pre-sell your company and products as well as ease the introduction of new products as you become more established.

Advertising

Selling – no matter how well your business is doing – selling will always be at the core of your business success. Mastering your sales skills ensures that those hard won potential customers are quickly changed to actual customers. Here are some selling skills to help you.

- **Answer the question** - "what is in it for me?" People buy to satisfy a need, a worry, because everyone else has it, or because they are curious about the product. Make sure that these questions are answered in your marketing and advertising as well as in any sales presentation.
- **Prepare yourself.** Get together your presentation as well as any potential questions you may be asked. Make sure that you have examples, pictures, samples etc.
- **Qualify your prospect** - make sure that they are the decision maker and can afford the potential purchase. Also, ensure that they are in your potential market - selling ice to Eskimos is for the expert of the foolish!
- **Develop a relationship** with your potential customers. People like to buy from friends and those that they trust.

- **Decide on your pricing structure** and build in some bonuses or discounts that you can offer during the presentation. Most people expect them.
- **Make the purchase process easy**. Make sure that you have any forms and contracts available. Do not surround your prospect with red tape or make it difficult to contact your company. Make the second and subsequent purchases even easier. Put a reorder form in the sales pack and make a subscription easy.
- **Ask for feedback**, directly or indirectly during your presentation and after the sale. AND learn from it.
- **Make the complete sales process fun** for both your customer and for you.

Lastly, make your advertising memorable and appropriate to your company.

Putting Your Business On The Internet

One advantage of doing business online is that you can start from scratch without investing much money. Here is a 25 Step Action Plan to help you get started...

1. Decide which of your services and products you want to include on your web site. Gather together your business information.

2. Brainstorm a list of keywords and phrases related to those hobbies and interests. For example, if you are going to sell small airplane collectibles, some possible keywords could be: airplanes, aeronautics, war airplanes, etc.

3. Research those keywords in Wordtracker.com to locate problem statements that have high search results and low competition. Wordtracker.com is a web page that helps you find out how many times your keywords are searched online, how popular your keywords on search engines are.

Those keywords may represent problem statements. Wordtracker shows you how many people are buying traffic on those keywords and how much are they paying. You need to find popular statements with low competition.

4. Research those problem statements further to determine if your products solve the problem stated. If not then tweak your products or change your keywords. You may use search engines to see how many people are offering products that can help to solve those problems. If you find a popular problem and there are not many people offering solutions online, you have got it!

5. Design your products based on previous research for you to sell. Once you found a hungry market, you just need to find the food that your customers want and they will eat from your hands. You may find companies online that can manufacture the products for you or you may find a different way to create the product yourself.

6. Write your sales copy for each product, establishing how you can solve the problems you have identified. Introduce your company and your business credentials. Write an "about us" page and a contact page.

7. Register a domain and set up a hosting account. There are many places online where you can register a domain and set up a hosting account in minutes. We use Godaddy and Hostgator - they are both leading companies that assist the beginner, but have enough to interest the more experienced business. Both have web templates you can use to give your business a professional look.

8. Register for a merchant account, to set up quickly use PayPal.com which is recognised everywhere. It can be a little bit more expensive, but it is a simple way to take credit card payments online very quickly.

9. Set up a simple web site using an automatic site builder or pay to have someone set it up for you. Do not try to design your own web site unless you are educated on html. Do not waste your time. Hire someone else to do it or buy templates that can be altered using MsFrontPage or MsWord. MsFrontPage is easy to use after a little practice.

10. Set up an opt-in form on your web site to collect e-mail addresses. You need to start collecting e-mail addresses for your newsletter. The major part of your business will come from the emails that you will send to your customer list.

11. Build an extensive keyword list based on the initial list of keywords you developed. Use Overture.com. For each keyword on the initial list, Overture can help you find different combinations with other words that you may find interesting. Check the popularity of each term and write down on a spreadsheet your final keyword list.

12. Submit those keywords to AdSense Adwords in order to start driving traffic right away. You need to start driving some traffic immediately in order to test your web site. The best way to do that is to buy this traffic at Google. Be very careful that you set a reliable budget and do not set your key words too wide.

13. Optimise and submit your web site to organic search engines (Google, Yahoo, AltaVista, etc...). Once you have proved that your web site works and sells, you will be ready to make the business bigger. It is then time to start working on building free traffic to your site.

14. Continue to test and tweak your web site until target conversion rate is met. Your conversion ratio should be that 1-2% of your visitors should buy from your web site, and 11% should subscribe to your newsletter. Continue testing until you get those stats.

15. Set up an affiliate program on your web site. Affiliate programs can double your business with no additional effort. Others will make the job for you. However, you cannot set up an affiliate program before you are sure that your web site can produce results. If your site does not work, you will loose your affiliates and they will never come back to you again.

16. Approach complimentary web sites to provide reciprocal links with you.

17. Start publishing a monthly newsletter. You have started collecting e-mail addresses much earlier, but it is not the time to start working the newsletter until you can prove that everything else works.

18. Submit articles to related newsletters and ezines on a regular basis. In the articles, you should always have a link to your site, so that you can get more traffic and you can get more people joining to your newsletter.

19. Continue the development of a content rich web site to further increase search engine rankings. Search engines love content. You must have many web sites which are rich on your keywords and which have links to your main page. A good way to do this is to add as many articles as you can, related to your business and link them to your home page.

20. Once keywords have been tested in Google Adwords enhance your marketing campaign - but always set a budget you are comfortable with.

21. Roll out tested keyword list in other major Pay Per Click Search engines. When you are sure about your stats, and you know how much money you collect per visitor, you must buy as much traffic as you can get as far as your income per visitor is higher than your bids.

22. Create a viral e-book to generate more leads. Create a free e-book that you can promote and that sells your product or service. Give it free, and this will bring more traffic to your web site.

23. Have an expert review and comment on your web site. Even if your site works, you can always improve. Listen to others and learn from their experiences.

24. Survey your existing customers to find out what other products or services they are looking for. Once you have a big list of customers, use it to find out what other problems do they have. Try to find or create a solution for them and you will boost your sales instantaneously.

25. Continue to test and tweak your web site and offers. Nothing is perfect the first time and can always be improved. It is very important that you take action, even if you make mistakes. Learn from your errors and improve your skills.

If you have read up to this point, you are probably asking yourself how much it will cost to get started. The answer is very simple; it depends on how much time and money you have available to invest! If you have a lot of time, you can do everything yourself. On the other hand, if you do not have time, you will have to pay other people to build your website and/or for optimising your site on search engines.

Chasing Work

You've been working with a potential customer and you think that you finally have the future project all worked out – then they ask you for a proposal. You have seen this great potential project but you need to bid for it. So how do you write that proposal that is going to win you the business?

Well first, let us look at what the proposal should do. Win of course, but before that, you have to:

- Make your company stand out from the others as well as reflect the values and Brand of your company.
- Offer the solution that is required in a format that is easily understood.
- Be well priced to attract the customer, provide a profit for your company as well as opportunities for you both to work together in the future.
- Be well structured, well written and well presented.

Bearing in mind the above, your proposal should look something like this:

4. 1) Thanks for the opportunity.
5. 2) Your understanding of the job that needs to be done.
6. 3) How you would complete the job, how long it will take and who will do it.

7. 4) Why your company is the best for the job.
8. 5) Your price - with subject breakdowns if appropriate.
9. 6) Any "must haves" assumptions made etc in getting to the price.
10. 7) Last thanks and way forward.

Item 5 and 6 should be on their own page so that they can be removed if necessary.

Remember to put your company details and contact details on the header of each page and your copyrights, date and page number and number of pages on each footer.

When you send off the proposal, on time of course, include a brief cover letter, with:

- Your contact details.
- The name of the person who is their contact for this bid.
- Your thanks for the opportunity.
- A very brief overview of bid - no price.
- A time frame that bid is current.
- Your thanks and hope to hear from them soon.

Now sit back and pride yourself on a job well done. Good luck.

Finding Customers

In order to establish your business and then increase your business and profits you have got to attract lots of customers and then get as much business from each of them as possible. This briefly is how a business works - without customers, you do not have a business!

Let us break that down to four easy steps.

- **Step 1:** Find your initial customers.
- **Step 2:** Make them so satisfied that they buy from you again.
- **Step 3:** Encourage your customers to spend more with you each time they buy from you.
- **Step 4:** Measure how effective you are in doing this and make sure that you do not lose those customers that you have.

We will give you a brief overview of each step now, and then in succeeding sections, we will look at each of them in more detail.

Step 1: Find Your Initial Customers

Potential customers are everywhere. You just have to find them. Here is a suggestion for starting small and building your customer base.

Get some samples of your new product made up in several different designs and colours. Use different fabrics if appropriate. If you have to use an external manufacturer, you may have to produce a minimum amount - so produce the most cost effective number and design options. Ensure you get a non disclosure agreement (NDA). Each sample should have your company and product name on it - either as a tag or stamped into it. This is to ensure easy product recognition when people take it away with them.

Go to an appropriate trade fair with your product and set up a stand. Have plenty of literature to hand out. You should be able to gauge interest here and hopefully take orders. If you wish to start slower or do not have the capital to do the trade show then start at flea markets, product parties and mall karts and work your way up.
Alternatively, approach potential retail companies with your success story. Start with the smaller ones and work your way up.

Networking - Why, How and Where

It is hard to be in business today, certainly in the professional services sector, without having heard the term 'networking'. Regarded by many as the Marmite of business, it is said that either you are a networker or you are not. In addition, if you think you are not, you should not even try to do it.

First, networking is essential to any business - whether offline or online. The business you get from personal recommendation will be some of the best business you ever do - they have pretty much made up their minds to use you before they even call you, and they are a lot less concerned with price.

It is not just for solicitors and accountants - when your pipes burst, how did you decide on a plumber to come out and fix it? Was it someone you had heard good things about before? Maybe you did not know anyone, so you called a friend and asked if they knew a good plumber. Joe Bloggs Plumbers just won the business of fixing your pipes through networking.

A good way to look at it is not as 'networking' but as 'word-of-mouth marketing'. Because it is part of your marketing mix - how is your advertising? Local papers? Spot on radio? Good, good. PR? Interview on local news this week? Fantastic. How about promotions? Give aways? Offers? All sorted? Great stuff. Got a website? Optimised for the search engines? Lots of enquiries from it too? Brilliant.

In addition, how about your word of mouth? Not enough people concentrate on generating referrals and getting people to mention their business to others. Millions of pounds of business is completed every year through referral and recommendation.

If you are not getting any of it, you need to think long and hard about why not.

So you have got yourself to a networking event, you tell the people there about what you have to offer, and then ask if they want to buy it, right? Wrong! If you do this, you have become the person at a networking event that everyone wants to avoid - the one handing out business cards as if they're dealing a poker game; the one that asks you nothing and tells you more than you could ever want to know about what they do.

So how do you do it? The best way to network is to build trust, build relationships, to think about what you can do for the other people in the room before you think about what you might get. Be a 'people person'; be genuinely interested in the people you meet at events.

Great networkers want to help as well as get help - because they like helping others, not just because it might get them some business in the future.

Networking is about building a relationship that eventually leads to business being done between either you or your new contact between you and someone they recommend or between them and someone you recommend.

Do not discount that last one - they have to get something out of your relationship as well, otherwise it is not a relationship. If you help them get more business, they will do the same for you - in fact, they will feel obliged to.

Where can you network? The short answer is absolutely anywhere! Remember Joe Bloggs Plumbers, the guys who fixed your pipes? You do not find many plumbers at networking events, but they still get referrals.

Networking happens when you talk to your colleagues at work, when you go to the pub with your friends, it happens when you overhear a conversation in the bus queue. Networking is about the impression you leave people with, and you make impressions all day, every day.

Of course, you will make more effective contacts for referrals at specialized networking events, but remember there are several different kinds of events you can go to. Some of the most established are breakfast meetings, which usually start around 7.00am and finish around 9.00am. Meetings are usually weekly and the format is very focused and regimented. For those who like this format, there is a lot of business to be done, but it is an acquired taste.

Try it out, but bear in mind whether or not you can keep up with the regular early mornings and very formal structure. In addition, most breakfast meetings are restricted to one person from each business sector, so you are not as likely to meet people you can form alliances and joint ventures with, which is a very important, and often overlooked part of networking.

There are also several different kinds of event organized by groups such as local government organisations, such as race days, golf days and others. These can be a lot of fun, but are very often filled with people who are there for the golf rather than to do business, and you may have to kiss many frogs to find your prince. Networking events are really a matter of preference and perspective, and you should go to as many events as you can at first, and then stick with the ones that work for you.

In summary, there is a simple and effective way to network that anyone can do:

- Get to know people as people, not prospects.
- Everything happens after a meeting, not during. Always, always follow up.
- Give referrals as well as expect to receive them.
- Keep in touch on a regular basis.

Step 2: Get Your Existing Customers to Buy From you More Often

It costs between six and eight times more to sell a new customer than it does to resell one of your existing customers. Therefore, selling to your existing customers repeatedly is actually more profitable than chasing new customers.

Here is why this is so powerful. Most customers are wary of not getting their money's worth when they make a purchase. Therefore, when they find a business that really delivers what it promises, that business stands out. Moreover, they are eager to buy from that business repeatedly.

Think about your own shopping experiences. Haven't you ever found some place that bent over backwards for you? You know what I mean, somewhere where you always get a great deal and great service.

How would you feel if that place sent you a letter and offered you a special deal on something? You would jump on it, wouldn't you? Well, as long as you have been taking good care of your customers, they will too.

Well, you are not alone. There are literally hordes of customers out there searching for businesses that really deliver value. Businesses they can trust. Businesses they can shower with repeat purchases. Become one of these businesses and you will quickly become successful.

Step 3: Encourage Them to Increase the Size of Their Purchases

This one sounds obvious, does not it? If you suddenly got your customers to increase the size of their average purchase by ten percent, your bottom-line would grow by ten percent, right? Wrong. It would actually grow by more than ten percent.

This is true because of a couple of things. First, your current level of business is paying for your fixed overhead, rent, salaries, utilities, equipment leases, etc. Therefore, any sales increases are more profitable since they do not add to your fixed overhead.

Next. when you combine this with getting your customers to buy from you more often, they will be spending more money with you -- and they will be doing it more often. The increase is actually compounded many times over.

Up Sell you way to a Better Turnover

Up selling - selling a more expensive but better item than the customer first wanted.

Simply show the customer a widget that's better, bigger, or faster than the one they was considering -- but with some special consideration such as a substantial discount, more favourable payment terms, extra options, or accessories.

If you become known as a business that delivers incredible values, you cannot lose. Remember, people cannot resist a bargain. Offer to sell the higher-priced model with a larger discount than the moderately priced one. Everybody wins here. The customer gets a much better value, and you get a bigger sale.

You are taking a smaller percentage of profit on the higher sale, but you are probably making more actual dollars. Plus, the customer is usually thrilled with the great deal. As you get a lot of business from word of mouth – this is a great way of getting even more sales.

Increase Your Sales With Just A Little Extra Effort

If you have steady sales but we just want to increase them a little more or maybe the problem you have is overstocking and you want to clear your inventory to free some of your cash flow. Here are a few suggestions for you.

- **Order Now:** You could offer your regular customers a coupon that provides them with a discount of a product if they order by "some date very soon". You could also use this in an advert by giving a code to quote when ordering or ask them to cut out and use the coupon. The magic words here are: "Instead of our usual price of $99, order by near date and get an instant rebate of $20, paying only $79!" What you have to ensure is that this is a genuine rebate – no one likes to feel scammed.
- **Mail In Rebate:** Similar to the order now option is a mail in rebate. Whilst this can be more labour intensive, it does improve your cash flow and provide you with names and mailing addresses that you can use in the future.
- **Samples:** If appropriate to your product, you can give out free samples to introduce it to and thus tempt other potential customers.
- You can do this a number of ways:
    - Sample tasting for food or drink items.
    - Sample chapters for books, MP3 or audio products.
    - Free short period phone consulting for services.
    - Free initial consulting for services such as legal, financial and medical.

- **Added Products:** Increase the perceived value of what you are selling by bundling other complimentary products with your original product. This can include such items as:
    - How To books
    - Consumables such as paper, ink, CD's etc
    - Extra consultancy or services on a complimentary subject – e.g. Personal tax return with business tax return or tooth clean with fillings.

- **Affiliate or Referral Selling:** If your product is appropriate and it is legal to do so, then offer others commissions for selling your products on your behalf. This can be done a number of ways:
    - Tempt others to sell for you by offering them a commission for every product they sell. You can deal with the delivery and fulfilment whilst they undertake advertising and managing the customer. This is very popular in the internet environment.
    - Offer commissions to people who refer customers to you. This can be money or products.
    - Sell your items via the party plan method – providing gifts or commission to the party host.

- Offer your existing customers 2 items for a lower price; they can then give one to friend or family member - thus increasing your customer base.

I hope that the above has given you some ideas. Yes, you will receive less for the extra products sold, but you will be increasing your customer base and your turnover. Good Luck

That is where the magic comes in. Make certain the customer is happy. Do not try to sell the customer something that is way out of their price range. They will end up resenting you for it. Do not get greedy! If you get greedy and try to "bleed" your customers, you will end up losing big in the long run. Just show them something that is slightly better that what they looked at first - do not pressure of hard sell. Let your offer speak for itself.

Once you maximize the value of each customer to your business, it is time to go out and get more customers. Now, every new customer you bring in is immediately and automatically worth more to you than before you implemented the first two steps.

Step 4: Measure How Good you are and Ensure they Remain your Customers.

If you have been in business some time - you will have more than one Marketing Strategy going on - so how do you find out which one is working?

Split testing is the answer. What is that? As this implies – you are splitting your campaigns and testing them separately. You do this by marking each of your marketing campaigns in some way so that you know where your traffic and sales are coming from and which campaign is the most successful. Here are a few ideas as to how to do this.

- Direct each campaign to a different company contact – be it web site, domain, email address or phone number. VOIP telephone numbers are very inexpensive these days as are domains.
- Give your customers a discount coupon and use a different coupon code for each of your campaigns.

- Use a slightly different mix of products for each campaign. Take care not to use different prices though as your customers might come from two different campaigns.
- If using Pay Per Click (PPC) then use your online account to separate each campaign.

Running through your receipts and web stats will soon tell you which is the most successful marketing campaign that you currently have running. Make changes to your campaigns as you feel the need. Use different by lines, headers, graphics and contents and experiment to see which campaigns have the best effect. Also, have a look at the products you are selling and the market that you are targeting. Often subtle changes are all that is required.

Remember, the longest journey begins with a single step!

Selling To Your Customers

No matter how well your business is doing – selling will always be at the core of your business success. Mastering your sales skills ensures that those hard won potential customers are quickly changed to actual customers. Here are some selling skills to help you.

- **Answer the question** - *"what is in it for me?"* People buy to satisfy a need, a worry, because everyone else has it, or because they are curious about the product. Make sure that these questions are answered in your marketing and advertising as well as in any sales presentation.
- **Develop a relationship** with your potential customers. People like to buy from friends and those that they trust.

- **Qualify your prospect** - make sure that they are the decision maker and can afford the potential purchase. Also, ensure that they are in your potential market - selling ice to Eskimos is for the expert of the foolish!
- **Prepare yourself.** Get together your presentation as well as any potential questions you may be asked. Make sure that you have examples, pictures, samples, brochures etc.
- **Decide on your pricing structure** and build in some bonuses or discounts that you can offer during the presentation. Most people expect them.
- **Make the purchase process easy.** Make sure that you have any forms and contracts available. Do not surround your prospect with red tape or make it difficult to contact your company. Make the second and subsequent purchases even easier. Put a reorder form in the sales pack and make a subscription easy.

- **Ask for feedback,** directly or indirectly during your presentation and after the sale. AND learn from it.
- **Make the whole sales process fun** for both your customer and for you.

Your Customers

The ability to know your customers provides you with a profit potential. Your first priority should be to know them and what they want and what they expect from your company or product. Knowing and understanding your customers increases the possibility of selling more goods to them, making them happier and thus increasing "word of mouth" advertising.

It is accepted business wisdom that a returning customer is the best customer. In a competitive market where the customer has a plethora of choices, returning customers indicate that they are satisfied with their first purchase and that they trust you. Therefore, a crucial part of your job in retaining your existing customers is to keep them thinking about your company and your products.

Interact with your customers and make records about their interests, wants and preferences. You can then provide customised products and information for their guaranteed satisfaction.

This type of marketing, which relies more on turning first-time buyers into loyal future customers instead of merely acquiring new customers, is called Relationship Marketing. One of the easiest ways to keep in contact with your customers is to send them a letter, email or newsletter.

Though it sounds simple, it helps in bringing many first time buyers back to a particular company. A few things that might be included in your customer communication, to induce customers to buy again are:

- **A sincere thank you:** welcoming customers to the company's services and assuring them that they are the most important part of a company.
- **A feedback form**: this enables the customer to directly offer their opinions on your services and products. This, in turn, may offer valuable suggestions to be kept in mind for new customers.
- **A general follow-up:** merely asking whether the customer is happy and satisfied with the product purchased helps in building up of customer faith.
- **A time-limited offer**: This introduces a sense of urgency in the customer's mind. Asking them to grab an offer within a particular time-period raises the customer's interest. Introducing the same offer in more than one letter with varying levels of urgency, each being more urgent than the previous one, makes the customer excited about the offer as well.
- **A "One Time Offer":** (OTO) is an offer that is only available at the time of purchase of another item. It makes the customer feel special and provides a sense of urgency.
- **Offering a Coupon:** to encourage customer loyalty and repeat business.

- **Additional references to other products**: particularly if the product is relevant to that which they have just purchased, shows that the company cares abut customer comfort and the personalised needs of the customer. To understand how powerful this is, this concept is recognised as being integral to the successful and meteoric growth of Amazon.
- **Asking the customer to refer the company:** to somebody they know, is also a good idea to promote not only customer faith but also introduces new buyers to your company. The customer might also be "rewarded" for their effort by giving them a discount on their next purchase.

Lastly ensure that you reply to customers making enquiries about their products and services very quickly, gaining a reputation of good service and excellent customer care.

Another simple and effective way to build relations with your customer is to send them greeting cards containing a simple expression of your appreciation for them. You could send out the cards for birthdays or anniversaries, on Christmas, Valentine's Day, or New Year. You could even use these cards as invitation to attend your special sales or for other more direct announcements.

Any company's main objective should be to promote a sense of security in the customer. It is important, therefore, that you make your customers feel comfortable, so that they keep coming back to your company, bringing in new references as well. After all, 'the customer is always right'!

Difficult Customers

Turning a Difficult Customer into a Customer that Comes Back: I really hate it when things do not go as they should and you have to spend time and effort sorting it out. I have hanging onto a phone line being told that "my call is important", when I have far better things to do.

Many companies are turning away possible loyal customers, because they do not know how to turn a complaining customer into a thankful customer who will come back to buy from you again. Here is our suggestion.

Firstly, I think that you have to put yourself in your customer's shoes – why do they consider it necessary to come into the store to complain? Then ask yourself, what will resolve your customer's problems?

If someone is angry or upset, it is because they feel injured or cheated in some way.

Your job is to let the customer vent and to listen attentively in order to understand the source of that frustration. When you do that, you send the message that you care about then and their problems.

If you treat the customer politely, understand what their problem is and give some kind of resolution to their woes – then you will have a happy customer again. Realistically though there are always some people who just like to complain or are complaining in order to gain something.

Firstly the No No's

- Do not lecture or talk down to your customer. I was once turned from annoyed to absolutely furious when instead of a refund for a fault on their side – I received a lecture on what I should have done instead.
- Do not promise things that you cannot produce – this will only escalate the problem.
- Do not be a "jobsworth" – that is do not suck the air through your teeth and say – "can not do that – it's more than my job is worth". Your role is to find a solution to the problem that your customer has.
- Do not stand over your customer – especially if you are a man talking to a woman or anyone talking to an elderly customer. This is intimidating.

- Alternatively do not be too timid either – they want to know that you are empowered to solve the problem. In addition, bullies will only feel that they can be more demanding.
- Do not lose your temper, become abusive or difficult, no matter how tempting – this will only escalate the problem.
- Anger is a natural, self-defensive reaction to a perceived wrong. If there is a problem with your company's product or service, some frustration and disappointment is justified. Do not fuel their anger by not understanding the complaint or not seeming to want to solve it.
- Do not try to cut them off, do not urge them to calm down, switch off from what they are saying, instead, and listen carefully to what the problem is.
- Do not question their understanding of the problem or question as to whether they have the correct dates/time/figures etc. Seeming to place blame onto the customer will only inflame the situation.
- Do not blame your company, or say "it's a common problem", not only will this annoy the customer more, but you open your company up to litigation or bad press.

Now The Must Do's

- Be polite at all times.
- Move to a quieter area of the store if possible – letting them know it is so that you can give them your total attention.
- If possible sit down with them – it is much harder to be annoyed when sitting and it also shows that you are there to spend time talking to them.
- Give them your name and assure them that you are able to solve their problem.
- Be confident and project a confident, caring attitude.
- Put yourself in the customer's place and try to see the situation from their perspective.
- Spend the first minutes of the conversation listening and being seen to listen.
- Once they have given you the details – summarize them back to them to show that you have understood.
- If you do not understand what the problem is – ask leading questions so that
- At this point your customer should be a little calmer and understanding that you are there to solve the problem for them.
- Apologize, emphasize and solve the problem.
- If it is a problem that is easily solved – such as a faulty item then offer a refund or exchange (depending upon your store policy) then solve it very quickly and with good grace and an apology!

- Offer a solution to the problem giving details of what you can do, when you will do it by. If it is not an immediately solvable problem then give an estimated time as to when it will be solved and take your customer's contact details.
- If store policy states that you cannot refund, make good or exchange, then find some other way of compensating them such as priority service, gift wrapping, credit notes etc. If this is not possible politely, explain why you cannot resolve the problem.
- **SOLVE THE PROBLEM.** Make the calls, contact the staff etc.
- Follow up with the customer as promised, giving updates as necessary.
- MOST IMPORTANTLY: Make the customer feel important, cared for and looked after. Let them know you are working hard to get their problem fixed.
- Thank them for their patience and understanding and assure them that you would love to see them back as customers.

REMEMBER: It is not whether or not you have a problem, or even what the problem is – the mark of a good business is how you solve the problems!

The Bad Customer

A bad customer is one that you do not want, but why on earth would you want to fire a customer? Well if they cost you more money and effort than the profit you make from them - then it is time for you to remove them from your mailing lists and your marketing activities. Here is 7 ways to recognise the bad customer.

1. The always quibble over prices - ensuring that your profit is minimal.
2. They are really slow to pay, costing your extra money in financing your cash flow.
3. They never seem happy with the service you provide and are keen to tell not only your staff but also other customers. Not only is this moral sapping for your staff, but damaging to your business.
4. They never refer any new business to you, never speak well of your company.
5. Their order has remained small and spasmodic.
6. They display no loyalty to your company and often go off to other companies for their orders.
7. They are very difficult to establish a working relationship with.

If you have customers that are displaying more than two of the above characteristics then you need to examine very carefully what profit and advantages keeping this customer is providing your company. However not all is lost.

There are ways that you can change these bad customers into better customers?

- Ensure that they understand exactly what level of service, cost structure and payment terms their account operates under.
- Try to address your customer's complaints on a once only attempt.
- Provide incentives to your customers to refer other business to you.

So, if all is lost and they are more of a problem to you than a profit, how do you get rid of the bad customers?

- Increase their costs by putting them on another pricing structure and decrease the payment terms. Similarly increase the delivery time.
- Remove them from your marketing strategies and mailing lists.
- If all else fails then write to them and politely remove them from your customer base, citing change of policies or similar.

Always be polite and remember – that a customer's complaints and late payment might be because you of how you have interacted with them! Maybe if you have too many bad customers you should be looking at that as well!

Setting Your Prices

When trying to sell your products or services pricing can be the single most important decision you will take. The pricing of products has to be done in such a way that the intended customers are willing to pay an amount that generates profit for the company or your business will not last long.

Since, the Internet provides a quick easy way to compare many of your competitors you need to ensure that your price is at the same level as your competitors. Of course they should compare like with like – so if you offer a better service or a more quality product, you need to emphasise this as well. These are called your differentials.

So first, you need to be aware if the prices that your competitors have set for similar services or products. So look for your potential consumers and then investigate the current prices they are paying.

Secondly, you need to estimate how much they would be willing to pay for your services or products. With any differentials that you have decided upon.

Lastly, you have to ensure that these prices are sufficient for you to make a profit. Sadly, this does not always happen.

Your costs are the sum total of the expenses that you incur when making a product. Expenses include cost of raw material, machinery, packaging, delivery etc. Price is amount customers have to pay for per unit of you product /service.

Obviously, your prices should be consistently above the cost if you are planning to run your company for a long time. Sometimes you can lower the prices, to gain entry into a market for example. Starting with prices, which are lower than your competitors, would make people notice you. In addition, once you collect a decent number of customers you can gradually increase prices! Similarly, you can lower your prices to see off a new competitor.

A Brief Word On Value

How much would customers pay for your services, is directly proportional to significant and valuable they think your product is. Of course your marketing strategies and reputation in the market will play a significant role in this regard.

One will never expect a high profile vehicle like a Mercedes to be priced at the same level as a Toyota for example or from a simple MP3 player compared with an iPod. In both these cases, value has been added to the product through good marketing as well as early research and development.

The simplest and most efficient strategy to satisfy a price sensitive buyer is to give them a vivid picture of the benefits their spending will get them in the long run. This is referred to as "selling the sizzle" of the steak as opposed to the steak!

Everybody likes to know that they spent good money on something that will last and give them the lifestyle that they aspire to.

Therefore, if you can convince your customer that buying from you is investing in something worthwhile and long term, they will agree and spend with you.

If you have a quality product and market it well any sane customer will come to you. Even if it means spending that little bit extra, customers want the best in the market for themselves. So providing quality products never fails to bring back customers for more.

So know your customers. Figuring out how their minds work and what they want will go a long way in convincing and wooing them to buy the right, even though more expensive, product.

In the end, the customer does not know, or care, if you are small or large as an organisation. she or he only focuses on the garment hanging on the rail in the store. ::: Giorgio Armani :::

Pricing Strategies That Improve Your Profit

Pricing strategies are a sometimes-overlooked part of marketing. They can have a large impact on profit, so should be given the same consideration as promotion and advertising strategies.

A higher or lower price can dramatically change both gross margins and sales volume that indirectly affects other expenses by reducing storage costs or creating opportunities for volume discounts with suppliers.

Six factors influence your pricing strategies:

- Your **competitors** and what they are charging for similar products.
- Your **suppliers** and who will supply wholesale items to you at what price.
- The **availability** of substitute products, that people might buy instead of yours.
- Your **customers**, where they are and what they are currently seeking.
- **Positioning**, which how you want to be perceived by your target audience. Price a premium item too low, for example, and customers will not believe the quality is good enough. Conversely, put too high a selling price on value lines and customers will purchase competitors' lower-price items.

Some pricing strategies to consider are:

- **Competitive pricing:** Keeping your prices at the same level as your competitors is the best way to do business. Stay alert about how much your next-door competitor is pricing their products and then price yours at a similar or lesser level to theirs.
- **Loss Leader:** Another effective strategy to woo customers and raise sales is to sell relatively cheap items at a lower price to customers who have the potential to buy more expensive things. This can only be a temporary arrangement and can often prove to be a gamble.

- **Cost plus mark-up:** This aims at fixing your prices according to your wish, as per the percentage profit you want to make and not the market pricing. this has the advantage of gaining you lots through setting cheap prices but this may also work adversely under certain circumstances. So think and decide wisely before setting the price.
- **Close out:** This is an interesting technique to try when you are clearing out your stock. This method involves selling your surplus goods at extremely cheap rates in order to prevent losses. By announcing this fact combined with a finite timescale and that these are the last that will be seen of them – you encourage buyers.
- **Bundling and quantity discounts.** The simple BOGOF – Buy One Get One Free always works well, except when your buyers just buy the same amount as usual! Give select customers a considerable discount on bulk purchases, either of the same kind, as in 5 shirts, or similar or related items. This is a good way to clear out stock that is getting to the end of its natural life as well as stock that that you are finding harder to sell. The masters of bundling are the fast food sellers who bundle burgers, fries and drinks together at reduced rates – so encouraging a bigger spend per buyer.

- **Uplifting:** A slightly different version of bundling is to offer upgrades or accessories at a cheaper price when buying the base item.
- **Trade discounting:** Short list the customers who can increase your profits and give them special offers so that they end up getting wooed into buying more from you and to keep coming back. Reduce prices, give discounts, do what it takes to get them back into your shop or office.
- **Versioning:** Putting different versions of the same basic product and then offering lower prices for the more basic models is a good way to sell to a new market and encourage them to buy from you again.

Pricing Policies

Pricing of goods is difficult. No single determinant magic formula exists that will decide the best price for one's product. There is no simple strategy but you can take certain measures to make more effective pricing policies.

Pricing policies are sometimes unnoticed as part of marketing .They can have substantial effect on profit, so should be given the same amount of thought as promotion and advertising tactics.

Variation in price can considerably change both gross margins and sales volume. This leads to indirect effects on other expenses by reducing storage costs, for instance, or creating
opportunities for volume discounts with suppliers.

Presented below is a framework for making pricing decisions that takes into account your costs, the effects of competition and the customer's perception of value.

- **Reward:** Your pricing strategy might take into account discount offers to consumers who offer you a business advantage. You may, for example offer cash discounts to customers who pay without delay. This system thus rewards those who help your company maintain a constant, positive cash flow and reduce credit collection costs.
- **Promotional allowances** frequently make economic sense. For instance, if your product is used in ad campaigns or in promotional activities by a retail chain that also sells your product it leverages your marketing efforts so offer them a discount.

- **Quantity:** Discounts for large orders makes economic sense when the cost-per-unit to sell or deliver a product reduces as the quantity sold increases. A caterer, for instance, may fill an order for 12 dozen cupcakes for one customer at 10 cents each, while cupcakes sitting in the bakery display rack may be sold to several customers throughout the day for 20 cents each. This is done because there is the probability that some of the cupcakes will not sell has to be considered. Costs are also associated with keeping the store open for random customers' convenience.
- **Trade-in allowances** for the return of old goods that one may either re-use or re-sell for a profit benefits both a company and consumers and encourages customer loyalty.
- **Seasonal discounts** reward customers who assist a company in balancing its cash flow and in meeting production demands during its quieter times.

Pricing as part of your Marketing Strategy

Pricing is certainly one of the most important factors in your Marketing Strategy. Correct pricing can make your product a hit or a failure in the market. The factors that have to be kept in mind when marketing your product are the following:

- It has to be of a quality that is acceptable to your market at the price you offer it at.
- It should have features that your buyers require or desire.
- It should be different from what your competitors have to offer and these differences should be apparent to your potential purchasers.
- It should be set at a good price point within the market.

Keeping these factors in mind, it is important to determine your pricing strategy so as to successfully sell your product in the current market conditions. Here are some pricing strategies that may fit well in your Marketing Strategy.

- **Generic or Economic Pricing:** This strategy is typically used by economic or generic (white label, own label) Brands and is often seen in the clothing market. The buyer is attracted by the low price and often does not expect the item to last long and so soon returns for the next version. For this strategy to be fruitful, you should have a low cost structure, minimal features and promotion and ensure you can quickly bring new items to market. Obviously, you should ensure that you reap some solid, stable benefits from acquiring customers in this manner.
- **Differential pricing:** In this method, the idea is to set the price according to different buyer types, e.g. the price will differ for an online store, a retail store and a departmental store; geographical area, by the quantity purchased; by national account segment, the price charged to a national account will vary from that charged to a local account. Do remember, there has to be a valid reason for applying differential pricing and adhere to any laws that may appertain.

- **Captive product or companion product pricing:** This strategy can be adapted to product line pricing as well. In this case, products are bundled together as companions and priced accordingly. (e.g. a mixer and mixing bowl). They also consider products as captives (e.g. a razor that can only be fitted with a particular blade). These products are often packaged in a single package, e.g. blades may be packaged with the razor. The prices of these products outside a package usually tend to be higher.
- **Premium pricing:** This strategy is applicable for luxury or high end goods such as expensive jewellery, yachts, planes, estates etc. You can use this strategy if the market recognises your product as a luxury or premium item.

Remember to review your products carefully before choosing a particular strategy so that the pricing is appropriate.

Increasing Profits

Running a business is hard work, and you do not always get back enough profit to compensate for the enormous amount of work that you undertake. Therefore, here are a few ideas on how to increase your profits.

First - do not be caught up in running your business and forget to continually review your progress and how you can improve. Take out your Business Plan and review what you set out to do and how you are progressing. Make any changes that you think will improve your business.

Take a little extra time on your Unique Selling Proposition (USP). Try to make it a unique and stand out from your competitors. Maybe also have a review of your marketing materials as well. Do they look tired? Old fashioned or just plain out of dates?

Next, look at your current market, has there been any changes, can you find any niches that you can climb into? Maybe your prices need a tweak here and there. Your target market has definitely grown up a little - have their requirements changed? Has new technology appeared? Match your current market against what you are selling into it and see if you can improve them.

Next - can you add to what people are buying - e.g. up sell. Fast food outlets up selling fries is the perfect example. Can you encourage your customer to spend just a little extra by offering them a natural extra bargain? Those extra pennies or cents add up over time.

Similarly, can you encourage your customers to upgrade their choice of product - maybe by making the price differential a little less?

Lastly, what else do your customers also buy when they buy your product? Do you sell it? Can you provide it or arrange with another business to provide it? These kinds of joint ventures are a win - win situation for both of you. Start incorporating other services that complement your existing business and watch the profits grow!

Just another thought, do you ask your existing customers for referrals? Providing discounts, coupons or commissions to them is a great way to painlessly grow your customer base.

Increasing Sales Whilst Cutting Back on Expenses

Let us look at the problem logically for a minute There are four basic ways you can increase your profits. You can:

1. Charge more for your products or services.
2. Sell more of your products or services to your existing customers.
3. Find additional customers.
4. Find ways to cut back on your business expenses.

We have already looked at the first three items earlier in this book so let us look at cutting back on your business expenses. If you are on a shoestring budget and who is not these days? Then obviously, you need to do everything you can to save as much money as possible, and make as much money as possible, as quickly and easily as possible. Here are some simple ideas you can use:

Know your target market. Who are your "ideal" customers? Where do they shop? What do they read? What solutions are they looking for that your business provides? The more you know about your customers, the better you will be able to target your promotions towards them, which will increase your bottom line two ways – it will save you spending money on advertising that does not work, and it will increase your sales, because you are offering your customers what they really want.

Get double duty out of any contact with your customers. If you sell products, put your contact information on everything -products, bags, invoices sales receipts. Make it easy for everyone to find you. Give away something free. If you have a Website (and if you do not, then get one), give your customers something for giving you their contact information. Free Ebooks, reports, or software are all good choices, just make sure it is relevant to your customers.

Anytime you send your customers anything - a product, a newsletter, an invoice -include a coupon or information about your latest products or services. To save money on postage, if you have a brick and mortar store, put a copy of your latest newsletter or an informational flyer in your customer's bag after each sale.

Reward your customers. Set up a reward program. Offer them a reward for anyone they refer who becomes a customer. Alternatively, give your customers a free gift when they spend $50 (or whatever amount makes sense in your business). When they are eligible for the free gift, offer them an upgrade to something bigger or better for a few dollars more. Start a customer loyalty program. Provide "customer only" sales, or promotions. Let your customers earn points, or "magic money" that they can use to redeem your products or services.

Get ready for your close-up. When you are brainstorming about creating a promotion or advertising campaign, do not forget about your local cable TV channel. You may be pleasantly surprised by how low their rates actually are. Create your own television commercial or infomercial. If this is too expensive look at recording a video for a social networking site. Internet radio is also reachable for those on a small budget. You can advertise on them or record your own podcast. Although you may not be ready for prime time, you can still target your ad to reach your customers.

Get involved in your community. Find a non-profit organisation that is doing work you believe in and either publicly support their program, or be one of their sponsors for an upcoming event or fundraiser. Use the advertising spot to let people know about the fundraiser (and, incidentally, your business). You could put together an inexpensive ad campaign that will help those in need, increase your visibility and let your potential customers know that you are supportive and aware of the needs of the community.

Get testimonials from your satisfied customers. However, do not stop there. What about creating your own television commercial that you can run in your store or on your web site. With a video camera and a little ingenuity, you could even create your own infomercial that shows customers how to use or get the most out of your products or services. If you have a web site, you can also put an audio testimonial on there.

Speak up. Again, keeping in mind who your ultimate ideal customers are and what their most pressing problems are, write an article, offer a free seminar, or offer to be a speaker at local chamber of commerce or other organisation or community meetings. Being perceived as an "expert" is a relatively easy and inexpensive way to get the word out about your business, and bring in more customers.

Create joint ventures. Even if your primary business is a brick and mortar one, you can still create a joint venture that will help you save money by sharing the costs for advertising. What about creating a special "sidewalk sale" with other business owners on your street or in your neighbourhood? Alternatively, finding businesses with complementary products or services to yours, and creating a "package deal"?

If your business is only online, look for ways you can partner with other businesses - maybe you could create solo ads and promote each other's products or services in your mailing lists. There are many ways you can save money and increase your customer base if you are willing to get creative.

Let your customers know you know what their problems are. It is sad but true that your customers do not care how good your products or services are. They only want to know two things: do you understand what their problems are; and can you solve them. Give your customers the "key" to their problems, and you will have evangelistic customers who come back again and again.

Administration

Administration is very important. Without good distraction your company will quickly disintegrate into chaos and you will not know who has what and who needs to pay for items and who needs them to be delivered. Your administration should include ways of controlling or managing the following:

- Managing your marketing materials - giving out, auditing, collecting, updating, refreshing. (Marketing.)
- Collecting orders and money from your customers. (Bookkeeping)

- Collecting purchased items from stock. (Fulfilment)
- Delivering purchased items to your customers. (Fulfilment)
- Banking money. (Bookkeeping)
- Managing returns. (Fulfilment)
- Managing enquiries and complaints. (Mailing)
- Invoice and bill payment. (Bookkeeping)
- Accounts and bookkeeping including, payroll, banking, taxes and VAT. (Bookkeeping)
- Purchasing and auditing stock. At least once a year and preferably quarterly, stock must be checked against your accounts. (Bookkeeping)
- Updating your web site. (Marketing)
- Salary and commission payments. (Bookkeeping)
- Staff training and development. (Staff)
- Product improvements and upgrades. (Research)

Bookkeeping

- Prepare and send invoices to customers
- Enter monthly transactions into bookkeeping programme.
- Reconcile bank, credit card, and other account statements.
- Enter in any payments received into your bookkeeping system.
- Send reminders for paying bills on their due dates.
- Write and prepare checks to be signed to pay bills.

- Daily or as required, send cash to bank.
- Monthly, reconcile your bank statement against your book keeping system.
- Quarterly or annually, depending upon your products, you should undertake a full audit of all your items and check them against you books.

It may seem a lot, but if you start small, get yourself a good accounts package, a good accountant, and bank manager it is a lot easier.

Managing your Mailing

- Retrieve email and mail, sort, and get rid of junk.
- Respond to sales requests immediately.
- Answer customer information and brochure requests as a matter of urgency.
- Respond to routine requests.
- Prepare packages and mail out products as orders arrive.
- Manage any payments received.
- Update your Customer Database.

Manage your Customer Database

To start with, you can use a simple card box system. As you get more customers, you can buy a suitable piece of software to assist you. There are called Customer Management Systems. When you obtain a new customer or prospect:

- Enter their details into a database or on the card.
- Send an introductory letter or emails to your new prospect leads. Alternatively, a Welcome letter to your new customer.
- Send scheduled marketing pieces to customers and prospects. If using emails you must use opt in permission marketing. In essence, this means – get their permission first.
- Track marketing efforts and summarize the results in a report. Your software will do this for you.
- Send regular follow-ups, reminders, and communications to customers. Make the information you send them pertinent and interesting.
- Track birthdays, anniversaries, and other important dates and end out the appropriate cards or gifts for special events.

Manage Your Marketing

- Design and print brochures and business cards.
- Create flyers, price lists, and other marketing documents.
- Lay out, printing, and mailing regular customer newsletters.
- Prepare professional-looking certificates for seminar participants.
- Print labels using company logos or clip art.
- Send out the appropriate sales brochures for inquiries.
- Create and mail a customer feedback questionnaire.
- Track the responses to this questionnaire.

Fulfilment

This is managing the process of receiving orders, sending out your products and managing your stock. It consists of the following:

- Collecting all orders together.
- Listing all your orders for the day.
- Checking orders against payments and producing invoices for those that have not paid and arrangements to pay later. Chasing the remaining payments required for all others.
- Collecting together the items ordered and paid or invoiced for. Tick them off your list.

- Put those ordered but not paid for on a pending payment list.
- Producing labels for all the items.
- Packing items with brochures and receipts. Labelling them.
- Mailing them out.
- Updating stock lists.
- Ordering stock as required. This can be done as a weekly or monthly basis.
- Collect returns together. If still sellable, put them back into stock and update stock list.
- Send replacement products to customer as required.
- Update book keeping as required.

Organize your Workspace

Your workspace, like your home, needs to be well organized. Use these handy tips to get your started: Organising your workspace:

- Use "L" and "U" shaped desks for the most efficient workspaces
- Store your gadgets and equipment -- telephone, computer, etc. on one "wing".
- Leave the other wing free to spread out while you work.
- Put your telephone on the side of the desk opposite your writing hand. This way you can hold the telephone and take notes at the same time

- Add a hutch for extra storage for books, supplies, and equipment.
- Avoid cluttering your workspace by filing away personal items.
- Do not hoard supplies at your desk but keep only what you need right now at your workstation and use a separate supply area for storing bulk amounts.
- Store away extras in labelled containers and group like items together.

General Office Administration

- Confirm upcoming appointments in your diary. Also, schedule or reschedule appointments.
- Get directions for a meeting or appointment.
- Back up computers for safe keeping.
- Renew necessary office supplies and ordering refills.
- Coordinate air travel, car rental, and hotel reservations.

Staff

- Train and development staff on a regular basis.
- Hold regular staff meetings.
- Employ staff as required.

Staff

As you expand you are going to need staff in order to undertake some of work in you business. In the beginning you can hire temporary or contract staff but as you become more established you will need staff that you can train and rely upon to work with your customers run the management and administration parts of your business.

You can hire staff from local job centres, job agencies, adverts and word of mouth. Just ensure that each new team member has the following:

- A job description and terms or reference that they understand and agree to. In this way, they know what their responsibilities are and what is expected of them.
- A company manual that explains your company, its products and services and where they fit in. Include an organisation chart if appropriate.
- Health and Safety manual. Many countries now insist on this.
- Suitable training for their new role.
- An introduction to their boss and staff.
- The appropriate uniform, office equipment and specialist equipment that they may need. This may include a computer account, email account, specialist tools etc.

- Details of where the important parts of the office/shop building are. This should include the toilets/restrooms, canteen, staff room, mailroom etc.

Motivating Staff

A Common Question I receive: I run a small party-planning company and I have been having some employee problems recently. It is difficult to find people who are qualified for the job, have customer service skills, and are easy for me to work with. Maybe it's just my bad luck, or maybe I'm not interviewing them properly, or maybe it's another problem that I'm not even aware of. How can an employer find people to do the job right!? Maybe it is all of them:

- Have you asked your staff why they want to leave you?
- Have you talked to your current staff and asked them for their advice?
- Do you have a training scheme to assist your staff in gaining the skills that you want from them?
- Is the way that the company works internally so difficult that people get discouraged?
- Can you do more to make your staff feel valued, wanted and part of the success of your company?

People work for a number of reasons that includes:

- The money obviously.
- To feel wanted and needed.
- For a sense of achievement.
- For companionship from other workers and customers.

You work in an environment where people are happy – are your staff? If you find out the answers to the above questions to your will an idea of why your staff are leaving so quickly.

So: Make your staff feel valued, happy and that they contributing to your business. Train them correctly and make your business run more efficiently and your staff turnover should reduce and your profits increase!

Looking After Yourself

An "Overload" Rescue Plan

At last, you have achieved your dream. You have escaped the traditional, away from home work force and are now self-employed.

There you sit, in your spiffy new office - whether it is in the corner of the sitting room or in a converted bedroom - surrounded by your equally spiffy new toys...your computer, desk and some strategically placed shelves.

Your new multi-function centre will print stuff, fax stuff and copy stuff. It will not hang out the washing, but hey, you cannot have everything.

You even have work coming in and the immediate worry about making a living has vanished. Hooray! You really can work from home!

At first, working at home is pure bliss. Then you get a week when everybody and their dog seems to want your services. After putting in a few late nights, you meet all the deadlines and think; phew...I am glad that is over! You decide to relax and give yourself a day off. After all, you worked all through the weekend and earned it, right?

Unfortunately, the following week you find yourself off to a bad start trying to make-up for your day off. Before you know it, you find that you are dropping further and further behind. You reflect gloomily that when you were working for someone else, at least at the end of the day you were finished...what didn't get done didn't get done!

Well, it is time to take heart and set a few simple strategies in place that will keep you in control of your time...and your sanity.

Do NOT Accept Any New Work This Week.

Take a good look at what you have on your plate now, and carefully plan the week ahead. Your aim is to regain control. Tell new customers that you are fully booked, but you can put them on a priority list to be phoned next week. (This will not only allow you to catch up, but make your services appear highly in demand.)

Build In Time For Leisure and Rest.

Not only for this week, but EVERY week. A half hour walk; a twenty-minute break in the sun with a cup of coffee; a quick swim or a movie outing with friends - all these activities can recharge your batteries. You will find that you can achieve far more when you are rested and alert. (How many times have you sat at the computer staring at the screen, achieving very little, because you are over-tired?)

Tackle Urgent Tasks First.

If you are behind, your first step must be to contact all customers and arrange firm new deadlines. Make sure you base these new deadlines on what you CAN achieve, not what you HOPE you can achieve. If any existing customer needs your services or products urgently, bump them up the line.

Prioritize Remaining Tasks.

Scrap anything that is not essential, and delegate what you can. Consider involving family, business associates or friends to handle some tasks. (Warning: do not hand over tasks that must be carried out only by you as the principal of the business. Your reputation is important.)

Set Achievable Daily Goals.

If you finish a task ahead of schedule, begin the next... but adhere to a definite cut-off time each day. What you are doing this week is establishing a system that will continue to work for you.

Getting out of trouble when your business is in overload is just like getting out of debt. Your business rating is similar to your credit rating - nothing can be gained by denying that a problem exists. Nothing can be gained by slipping deeper into the mire. Call a halt; contact the main players; set workable strategies in place and you can quickly regroup.

Expanding Your Company

What can a small or medium business do to break through that plateau phase that most of us hit? If you have good annual sales but feel like it is time to grow larger. Should you be pouring lots of money in to marketing? Alternatively, should you up production? Alternatively, is there something else you can do?

First of all congratulations on establishing your business and being ready to reach the next level – which is often the more difficult stage where some fall foul of their ambitions. This is really a situation where we would you should to sit down with your advisors and discuss your specific business but here are some areas that you should be looking at:

- **Expand into other geographic areas.** Do you have customers that are regularly coming to you from a specific area – if so look at placing an outlet there?
- **Expand your product range.** Are you regularly asked for something you do not do? Do some of your customers make do with what you can provide them with? Do you see and opening for another service or product? If you research and plan how to meet these needs?

- **Become more efficient.** Have you become a little lazy in your processes and procedures? Is what you are doing fine when you are small, but a little cumbersome now? Small changes and improvements can sometimes pay big benefits – ask your staff who are close to the methods what they suggest.
- **Review your prices and profits.** Are they in line with your peers and competitors?
- **Improve your marketing.** Is there something you want to tell people about your business or products? Are you reachable via your website, email and free phone? Have you made a press release lately? Do you have a Marketing Strategy?

You need to sit down, with or without an external consultant, and produce the following:

- **Your Business Plan** for the next 3 years, showing your business strategy, what you wish to sell, to whom and for how much and how you want your business to be perceived by your customers, peers and competitors.
- **Your Marketing and Advertising Strategy.** How much you have to spend, on what and to whom you wish to sell. You should identify what makes you unique and what your company Brand looks like.

Franchising

If you have a business that can be duplicated in many different regions why not consider setting your business up as a franchise. Similarly, if you have a business with numerous outlets why not franchise some of these? Alternatively why not turn your head office location into a franchise headquarters and then sell off franchises?

This option does take some time and money to set up. It can drastically decrease the time that you have to spend with your business, whilst still providing a good income or it can take your business into a completely new direction. Just ensure that your core Business Model and business processes are strong and viable before you take the plunge!

Investment to Expand

Angel Investors are considered by many to be the best type of investor in your business. Angels are usually successful business owners and entrepreneurs who can also bring you valuable industry experience, executive knowledge, creative ideas and contacts. They can usually afford to indulge their love or risk and are often seeking new business challenges. To be an angel in the USA, one must be an "accredited investor," which the Securities and Exchange Commission defines as someone with a net worth of at least $1 million or an annual salary of at least $200,000. Similar rules exist in other countries.

So how do you attract and investor to your business and are they really what you want?

Build a Convincing Case: Angel investors may be willing to take on more risk than most, but they still need to see a well thought out Business Plan with a proven product that has a recognizable and eager market need backed by a competent management and development team.

Establishing Your Market: Your angel will need to be convinced that your business will meet the market need and that there is a clear "barrier to entry" from competing companies. They will hardly want to invest in your company only to see your marketing advantage disappear. Typical barriers to entry are: patents cost of development and proprietary processes.

Your Management Team: Angels they will want to know that their investment is in safe hands. They will want to know the quality and experience of your managers and that they are all committed to your company.

A Great Business Plan: This defines your business, market, potential customers and your goods and services as well as the strength of your management team. It lets your angel have a good idea of your financials and how they will profit from investing in your business. Your Business Plan is not only a great selling tool it also assists you in planning and developing your business, placing it on a firm foundation. Consider using a professional Business Planning service for this. Not only will they work with you in producing a great Business Plan, but a good company will identify your business weaknesses and suggest better ways to do things.

Use a good Business Planning company – that is not one that charges less than $500 – you will get a plan and nothing more. Look for a company that charges a rate that allows them to offer you consultancy, advice and assistance as well.

Put Your Money where your Mouth is: If you want to start a business, be prepared to invest your own money. Entrepreneurs, who expect angels to risk money in their venture, should be as confident about their own money. Entrepreneurs who are not willing to assume such a risk are not considered serious by investors and will probably not receive funding.

Find the Right Angel: Angels typically invest in companies that they know something about. Identifying appropriate angels will increase your chances of success. When pitching, ask them what they look for in a company, how much they typically invest, what kind of return they expect on their money.

Expect the Angel to be Involved: Entrepreneurs should also be choosy about whom they take money from. Make certain that you really know your Angel, understand their motivation and expectations for exit strategy and ROI (return on investment).

Your angel will probably want a seat on the board and definitely a say in how you spend their money. Be prepared for this – not only do they need to protect their investment but they also will have knowledge and experience that your company will greatly benefit from. Being able to answer angel questions without feeling threatened is crucial to building a professional and mutually profitable relationship. Knowledgeable angels with good connections can jump start a company and keep it thriving. Well-connected angels can even make it easier to get additional rounds of financing including venture capital.

Professionalism Persistence and Patience: Raising capital is a time-consuming, ego-challenging process. It is not unusual for a start up entrepreneur to spend 50%-70% of his time raising capital from Angel Investors, a process that can average 3-6 months and in an uncertain market, it take even longer. Efforts to horde stock, inflate valuations or produce unbelievable financials will make the company less attractive to suitors.

Let experienced professionals - produce your financials and manage your legal activities.

Lastly, entrepreneurs must be determined, passionate about their business and thick-skinned.

Angel investors are not so concerned with you going public, but are still looking for a quick and high rate of return on their investment. They are not as sophisticated as venture capitalists or institutional investors and are more likely to wish to be in your business.

Venture Capitalists

If you now have a large company and are looking to expand rapidly then you should be looking at attracting a Venture Capitalist. Venture capitalists understand risk very well. When reviewing your Business Plan - you do have a Business Plan don't you? They are asking three questions:

1. How risky is this business for me to invest in?
2. What is in this for me - e.g. how much can I earn for investing in this business?
3. When can I profitably cash out of this business and move onto another?

Answer these three questions in your Business Plan by showing that you have mitigated and minimized your risks by undertaking extensive research.

Show what the return for the investor is likely to be and please make it believable. Show them how they can leave your company with a smile on their face and a good return for risking their money in believing you.

Venture capitalists actually are quite happy to invest in good well thought out and planned new companies. However all new businesses are not equal - here are the less popular types of companies:

- Internet only companies – especially if you obviously have no idea how to market it and are not supporting the business with conventional advertising and marketing.
- Any business where you ask them to take a share of the profits and do not offer them a stake in the business.
- Businesses that have been done hundreds of times before – there are only so many coffee shops that a city can support.
- Any business where you are personally not making a financial investment – if you do not want to invest why should they.
- Any idea that is poorly thought out poorly planned or simply will not work.

Please remember that venture capitalists are seeking high returns in exchange for their high risk investment. Many of them expect your company to go public within a short time frame.

Remember venture capitalists are not the only way to raise business investment. Your first port of call for business investment should always be the bank, SBA and relatives.

Selling Up

Many business owners either with a new or established business are seeking to capitalize on their hard work and move onto other things. Some entrepreneurs are seeking capital from Angel Investors and need to provide suitable exit strategies within their Business Plans. Here are a few Exit Strategies for you.

- **Sell:** The most obvious option if you have a viable business.
- **Asset Strip:** You can pay yourself a huge salary and sell off all viable components of the business. It could be that this is a more profitable option than selling your business as a going concern.
- **Minimize the Business:** If time is your problem then just restrict your trading hours and/or product line. Outsourcing some areas of the business will give you more time.
- **Liquidation:** Cease trading, pay off your debts and sell your assets. Close the doors and walk away with your memories and stories.
- **Give your Business Away:** You can remove yourself from the business and leave your business to your heirs. Take legal and financial advice first though please.

Here are a few more conventional exit strategies that an investor will be interested in hearing about.

- **Consultancy:** You could let your management team take over the running of the business and take on a consultancy or executive role. This can only be done if your management team are capable of running and improving your business. This option is quite often take if you personally have reached the pinnacle of your ability, or want to spend more time away from the business. This option allows for a more experienced management team to run the business whilst you retain an income and influence on the business. An example of this would be Anita Rodderick of Bodyshop – who took the opportunity to follow her love of conservation whilst still retaining some influence over the company that she founded.
- **IPO:** The holy grail of business and one that you read about when people become "over night millionaires". About as likely as becoming an overnight millionaire by winning the lottery. Unfortunately rather than handing over your Dollar/Pound/Euro for a ticket – you are going to spend hundreds of thousands on lawyers, analysts, PR and bankers!

- **Merger or Acquisition:** This is a particularly attractive option when you are a small company with a strong presence in a niche market. There are many small company owners that have become very rich by being bought out by the likes of Google or Amazon. These large companies do this as they want the products you have and buying a company is cheaper than the research and marketing necessary to bring these products to market. The merging or acquiring company is paying for your assets, patents, copyrights, good will, market share and customer base. In a merger you can arrange for a nice consultancy post for yourself in exchange for giving up your chairmanship. Not quite giving up the business but not a bad lifestyle.

Whichever option you choose – choose carefully and good luck with your new found wealth and leisure.

If you need any advice about planning and setting up your business then contact The Biz Guru at www.BusinessPlanNow.com

Start up Business Advice can be found at www.StartNewBusiness.com

Good luck with your New Business.

Index:

www.ingramcontent.com/pod-product-compliance
Lightning Source LLC
Chambersburg PA
CBHW031812190326
41518CB00006B/303
* 9 7 8 1 9 0 7 5 5 1 0 4 8 *